# MAKING

# LIQUEURS

# AT

# HOME

- inexpensive
- fun
- easy
- completely legal

*Compiled by* **Carmen Patrick**

Making Liqueurs at home — a delightful hobby that will give you great pleasure, and will save you money. This pastime has been steadily growing in popularity as more and more people learn the art, and create new recipes. Yet, as I have discovered, there are few published books on making liqueurs.

With this in mind I began gathering recipes and information about liqueurs. This book is a compilation of contributions from friends, family and other books whose recipes I have greatly enjoyed. Many have also been gathered during travels in other countries.

It will give you many ideas on how to make and serve liqueurs. Impress your friends with recipes from this book, or create your own combinations. All are fun, easy, and inexpensive!

Many thanks to those who have contributed recipes to this collection. Special thanks to my mom for without her, this book would not have been a possibility.

### Enjoy!

*Carmen Patrick*

# TABLE OF CONTENTS

RECIPES:

| | |
|---|---|
| Almond Liqueur | 4 |
| Amaretto Liqueur | 6 |
| Anisette Liqueur | 8 |
| Apple Liqueur | 9 |
| Apples in Liqueur | 9 |
| Apple Tea | 10 |
| Apricot Liqueur | 12 |
| Artichoke Liqueur | 14 |
| Artichoke and Brandy | 14 |
| Banana Liqueur | 16 |
| Bay Leaf Liqueur | 18 |
| Blackberry Brandy | 18 |
| Blackberry Liqueur | 19 |
| Blackberries in Liqueur | 19 |
| Black Currant Brandy | 21 |
| Blueberry Liqueur | 22 |
| Cafe Sport | 23 |
| Camomile Liqueur | 24 |
| Cantaloupe Liqueur | 25 |
| Caraway Liqueur | 26 |
| Cherry Brandy | 27 |
| Cherry Liqueur, Black | 27 |
| Cherry Leaf Liqueur | 28 |
| Cherry Liqueur | 28 |
| Chocolate Liqueur | 30 |
| Coconut Liqueur | 30 |
| Clear Orange Liqueur | 31 |
| Coffee Liqueur | 32 |
| Creme de Cacao Liqueur | 33 |
| Creme de Menthe Liqueur | 34 |
| Cream Marsala | 36 |
| Curacao | 37 |
| Drambuie | 38 |
| Egg Liqueur | 39 |
| Eggnog Liqueur | 40 |
| Four Fruits Liqueur | 41 |
| Galliano | 42 |

| | |
|---|---|
| Gooseberry Liqueur | 43 |
| Grapefruit Liqueur | 43 |
| Green Grape Liqueur | 44 |
| Green Grape Vermouth | 45 |
| Green Tomato Liqueur | 46 |
| Huckleberry, Elderberry or Bilberry Liqueur | 47 |
| Huckleberries, Elderberries or Bilberries in Liqueur | 47 |
| Irish Cream | 48 |
| Juniper Liqueur | 49 |
| Kirsh | 50 |
| Kummel | 51 |
| Lemon and Orange Liqueur | 52 |
| Milk and Cherry Liqueur | 53 |
| Moka | 54 |
| Mountain Ash Liqueur | 56 |
| Orange Brandy | 57 |
| Oranges in Liqueur | 58 |
| Orange Liqueur, Dry | 59 |
| Orange Liqueur, Sweet | 59 |
| Orande and Lemon Liqueur | 60 |
| Orange and Pear Liqueur | 60 |
| Peach Liqueur | 61 |
| Pear Liqueur | 62 |
| Peppermint Liqueur | 63 |
| Pineapple Liqueur | 64 |
| Pineapple Rum | 64 |
| Plum Liqueur | 65 |
| Plums in Liqueur | 65 |
| Pomegranate Liqueur | 66 |
| Raspberry Liqueur | 67 |
| Raspberries in Liqueur | 67 |
| Rhubarb Liqueur | 69 |
| Rose Liqueur | 70 |
| Strawberry Liqueur | 71 |
| Tangerine Brandy Liqueur | 72 |
| Tangerine Liqueur, Dry | 72 |
| Tangerine Liqueur, Sweet | 73 |
| Tangerine Vermouth | 73 |
| Vanilla Liqueur | 74 |

# About Liqueurs

The history of making liqueurs goes back almost 2,000 years. It was not until the Middle Ages though, that liqueurs came into general use. They were developed by the alchemists, monks and sorcerers of that period. Monks, whose monastery gardens provided the raw materials, were the chief experimenters.

The first liqueurs were used as medicines and aphrodisiacs. The medicinal qualities of some liqueurs are well established, especially those made from coriander, caraway seeds and various roots and herbs.

# How Liqueurs Are Made

About the only thing easier than making liqueurs, is drinking them. They require no special equipment, skill or culinary talent — just a bit of patience.

Liqueurs are generally divided into two categories; those made with plants, and those made with fruits. Although there are various methods for making liqueurs, this book only gives recipes for two basic methods; "by scratch" using the steeping method, and with "extracts" — the addition of a flavor extract.

To steep, all you do is put the various ingredients in an alcohol base for a specific period of time. Sweeteners are added for palatability. After this period, the liqueurs are filtered until clear, bottled, and then set aside to mature before serving. Instructions for making these scratch liqueurs are included with each individual recipe.

The Extract Recipes simply involve adding the flavouring extract to the spirit. The extracts that I have found to work extremely well, and use in this book, are those made by the T. Noirot firm of Nancy, France. By using these extracts, which can be found in wine making supply shops, the liqueurs can be served the same day they are made. Of course, like all liqueurs, these too improve with age.

Extract liqueurs are easily made. All you do is make a simple syrup of 2 parts sugar to 1 part water. Add the Glucose Solids, also available in wine making shops, to this mixture and boil slowly until dissolved. When this cools, add the flavouring and spirit. To mix ingredients more thoroughly, blend them in a blender for a short time. Then bottle the liqueur, let settle and enjoy!

For recipes which do not require a simple syrup, mix the ingredients well in a blender.

In making your own liqueurs, you can determine the strength wanted by using a 40, 80 or 100 proof spirit. The sweetness, flavour and color can also be adjusted to your taste.

# Equipment Needed

Most, if not all of the equipment for making these liqueurs can be found in your kitchen. The items include:

- a small saucepan
- a blender
- cheesecloth or cloth
- tight sealing glass jars
- measuring utensils - cups, spoons, etc.
- paper filters
- a colander or strainer
- a funnel

# General Hints

It is best to use fresh fruit and vegetables, washing them well.

Make sure the jars and bottles are clean and sterilized.

Dissolve the sugar in boiling water unless otherwise stated.

Make sure the jar is always tightly closed, or the bottle firmly corked.

Label the jars and bottles with the name and date.

Store all liqueurs in a cool place away from bright light.

For those liqueurs which are stored for several months, it is wise to seal the lids with wax.

# Abbreviations Used

| oz. | = | ounce |
| T. | = | tablespoon |
| tsp. | = | teaspoon |
| lb. | = | pound |
| " | = | inch |

# Almond Liqueur

Two great recipes!

This clear liqueur has a delicate almond flavour.

| | |
|---|---|
| 2 | lbs. diced almonds |
| 2 | cups sugar |
| 1 | cup water |
| 4 | whole cloves |
| 2 | cups vodka |

Put almonds, cloves and vodka in a quart jar and cover. Steep for **6 months** and then strain. Boil water and sugar until dissolved. When cool, add to almond mixture, stir and leave until clear.

This sweet, rich liqueur is made with a base of almond milk. There is a light and delicate almond aroma which is faintly touched with spices.

| | |
|---|---|
| 2 | cups almond milk |
| ½ | lemon - yellow peel only |
| 4 | whole cloves |
| ½ | inch piece cinnamon stick |
| ¼ | tsp. caraway seeds |
| 1¼ | cups sugar |
| 1¼ | cups water |
| 2½ | cups vodka |

Slice lemon peel, and place in a tightly sealed jar with cinnamon, cloves, caraway and vodka for **5 days**. Dissolve the sugar in boiling water, cool, and add it to the contents of jar. Mix well, let stand for **2 more days**, and then add the almond milk. Mix thoroughly and let stand for **15 more days** in a cool, dark place. Filter through cheesecloth and return to cool, dark place for **1½ months**. Filter once more to remove the sediment and enjoy!

Almond milk can be prepared by shredding 6 oz. of blanched almonds in a blender. Combine with 6 oz. of sugar, and 12 oz. of distilled water. Shake mixture until sugar is dissolved.

## Extract Recipe:

| | |
|---|---|
| 2 | cups sugar |
| 1 | cup water |
| 6 | T. Glucose Solids |
| 1 | bottle Almond Extract |
| 2 | cups vodka |

# Amaretto Liqueur

A smooth, golden brown liqueur with a rich almond flavour.

2 cups crushed peach pits
½ tsp. ground coriander
½ tsp. ground cinnamon
2 cups sugar
1 cup water
2 cups vodka

Steep the vodka, spices and crushed pits for **2 months**, then strain. Boil the sugar and water until dissolved. Cool and add to peach pit mixture. Leave until clear.

### Extract Recipe:

2 cups sugar
1 cup water
1 bottle Amaretto Extract
2 cups vodka

## How To Serve:

### Amaretto and Tea

Add 1 oz. amaretto to hot tea.

### Blueberry Tea

Add to hot tea.

¾ oz. amaretto
¾ oz. orange brandy

## Latin Lover

Pour over ice:

¾  oz. amaretto
¾  oz. moka
    cream

## EXTRA!

## Floating Liqueurs

To float liqueurs, pour each one over the blade of a knife, making layers. Pour the heaviest or the sweetest liqueur first.

# Anisette Liqueur

This liqueur has a strong licorice flavour.

| | |
|---|---|
| 5 | T. crushed anise seed |
| 1½ | tsp. crushed fennel seed |
| 1½ | tsp. ground coriander |
| 1 | cup honey |
| 3 | cups brandy |

Combine the brandy and spices and steep for **3 weeks**, shaking the jar occasionally. Strain through a cloth a few times, and stir in honey. Let stand until clear.

**Extract Recipe:**

| | |
|---|---|
| 2 | cups sugar |
| 1 | cup water |
| 1 | bottle Anisette Extract |
| 2 | cups vodka |

## How To Serve:

**Jelly Bean**

Float:

| | |
|---|---|
| ½ | oz. tequilla |
| ½ | oz. anisette |
| ½ | oz. grenadine |

# Apple Liqueur

This is a delightfully light liqueur with an extremely pleasant taste.

| | |
|---|---|
| 6 | cups chopped apple |
| 1 | cinnamon stick, broken |
| 1½ | cups sugar |
| 3 | cups brandy |

Combine all the ingredients in a tightly covered jar. Invert the jar and let stand **24 hours**. Turn jar upright, and let stand for **24 more hours**. Repeat the turning process until sugar dissolves. Store in a cool, dark place for **2 months**. Strain through cheesecloth and enjoy!

For a more interesting flavour, add the peel of 1 whole lemon or 2 whole cloves, or combine the two together.

# Apples in Liqueur

Tasty pieces of apple steeped in a lightly spiced liqueur.

| | |
|---|---|
| ½″ | piece cinnamon stick |
| 2 | leaves lemon verbena |
| 6 | whole cloves |
| 5 | apples |
| 1 | cup sugar |
| 2½ | cups vodka |

Cut the apple into large pieces (do not peel). Add apples, sugar and ½ cup of vodka to a tightly sealed glass jar. Let sit in sun for **1 week**. Add remaining ingredients and mix gently. Let steep for **7 months** in a cool, dark place. Save apples for a delicious dessert.

# Apple - Tea

This liqueur has the appearance of brandy but a taste which is uniquely its own.

|      |                       |
| ---- | --------------------- |
| 1    | tsp. tea leaves       |
| 1    | tsp. hibiscus petals  |
| 1    | tsp. camomile blossoms |
| 1    | apple, quartered      |
| 1½   | cups sugar            |
| 2    | cups water            |
| 2    | cups vodka            |

Boil the tea, camomile and hibiscus for 6 minutes in half of the boiling water. Dissolve sugar in remaining water, cool and add all the ingredients to a tightly sealed glass jar. Steep for **15 days**, shaking occasionally to mix ingredients. Filter through a cheesecloth and store in a cool, dark place for **5 months.**

## How To Serve:

### Saucy Sam

Stir well and strain into a glass:

|     |                      |
| --- | -------------------- |
| ½   | apple liqueur        |
| ½   | brandy               |
| 1   | dash apricot brandy  |
| 1   | dash pernod          |

Garnish with orange peel.

## Sledge Hammer

Shake with ice and strain into glass:

      1/3  apple liqueur
      1/3  brandy
      1/3  rum
      1     dash pernod


## Tender Bill

Shake with ice and strain into glass:

      ¼    apple liqueur
      ¼    apricot brandy
      ½    gin
      1    dash lemon juice

# Apricot Liqueur

Two great recipes!

A very popular fruit liqueur.

| | |
|---|---|
| 10 | T. thick apricot jam |
| 2 | T. honey |
| 3½ | cups brandy |

In a blender whip the jam and brandy. Put in a tightly sealed jar and store in a warm spot for **6 weeks**. Strain through a cloth and add honey, mixing well. Leave until clear.

This recipe has a tangy flavour when it is made with dried apricots and a mild, delicate flavour when made with fresh apricots.

| | |
|---|---|
| 2½ | cups fresh apricots, or |
| 1½ | cups dried apricots |
| 6 | crushed almonds |
| ½ | inch piece cinnamon stick |
| 1½ | cups sugar |
| 2½ | cups vodka |

For fresh apricots, pit the fruit and remove seeds from the pits. Crush the seeds and mix with apricot pulp. Place in a tightly sealed jar and add remaining ingredients.

For dried apricot: cover in water until plump. Crush the almonds and add to drained apricots. Add remaining ingredients and put in a tightly sealed jar.

In both cases, let stand for **3 weeks**, shaking occasionally. Strain through a paper filter into a glass jar and seal tightly. Let stand for **7 months** in a cool, dark place.

**Extract Recipe:**

- 2    cups sugar
- 1    cup water
- 1    bottle Apricot Extract
- 2    cups brandy

# How To Serve:

### Boston Cocktail

Shake with ice and pour into a glass:

- ¾    oz. apricot liqueur
- ¾    oz. gin
- ½    oz. grenadine
- ¼    oz. lemon juice

# Button Hook
Shake well with ice and strain into glass.

- ¼    oz. Pernod
- ¼    oz. apricot liqueur
- ¼    oz. brandy
- ¼    oz. white creme de menthe

### Fifth Avenue
Pour over ice:

- 1    oz. apricot liqueur
- ½    oz. cacao
- ½    oz. cream

# Artichoke Liqueur

This liqueur can be served both as a tasty apertif and a satisfying after dinner drink.

| | |
|---|---|
| 20 | artichoke leaves |
| 1 | basil leaf |
| 1 | sage leaf |
| 1 | tsp. caraway seed |
| 4 | coriander seeds |
| 2 | whole cloves |
| ½″ | piece cinnamon stick |
| 1 | lemon - sliced peel only |
| 3½ | cups sweet red vermouth |
| 1 | cup vodka |

Mix artichoke leaves, vermouth and vodka together in a tightly sealed jar. Leave for **2 days** and then strain. Add remaining ingredients and leave for **1 week**. Pour through a paper filter into a glass jar, seal tightly and let mature in a cool, dark place for **3 months**.

# Artichoke and Brandy

This liqueur has a pleasant bouquet and can be served with lemon as an apertif.

| | |
|---|---|
| 20 | artichoke leaves |
| 2 | whole cloves |
| 2 | cups dry white wine |
| 2 | cups brandy |

Let artichoke leaves, cloves and brandy sit in a tightly sealed jar for **2 days**. Add wine, shake well, and let sit for another **2 days**. Strain through a paper filter into a glass jar, seal tightly and store in a cool, dark place. Leave for about **4 months**.

**EXTRA!**

Do not worry about liqueurs going bad. If sealed and stored properly, the longer they sit, the better they taste!

# Banana Liqueur

A highly flavoured, golden liqueur from the Caribbean.

| | |
|---|---|
| 1 | medium sized ripe banana |
| 1 | cup sugar |
| ½ | cup water |
| ¾ | tsp. vanilla extract |
| 3 | cups vodka |

Mash the banana and place in a glass jar. Add the vodka, closing the jar tightly. Let steep for **8 days** and pour through a strainer to remove most of the banana. Add the sugar syrup and strain again to remove remaining haze. Add vanilla and stir. Leave for **1 more week**.

This rich, sweet liqueur is delicately flavoured with spices.

| | |
|---|---|
| 5 | medium sized ripe bananas |
| 3 | whole cloves |
| ½" | piece cinnamon stick |
| 2½ | cups sugar |
| 1 | cup sweet red vermouth |
| 2 | cups vodka |

Cut bananas into ½" slices and put into a tightly sealed jar with sugar and vermouth. Leave for **10 days** and then add remaining ingredients. Mix well and store for **1 month** in a cool, dark place. Strain through cheesecloth until clear and store again in a cool, dark place. Leave for about **2 months**.

**Extract Recipe:**

>    2    cups sugar
>    1    cup water
>    1    bottle Banana Extract
>    2    cups vodka

# How To Serve:

**Banana Cow**

Blend and pour over ice:

>    1    oz. banana liqueur
>    1    oz. simple syrup
>    1    oz. light rum
>    1    oz. cream
>    ½    oz. lime juice
>    ½    banana

**Banana Sandwich**

Shake and strain over ice:

>    ¾    oz. banana liqueur
>    ½    oz. creme de cacao
>    Fill glass with cream.

# Bay Leaf Liqueur

This liqueur has a pleasant bouquet and is particularly appropriate and delicious after a fine dinner.

    30    whole bay leaves
    1¾    cups sugar
    1¾    cups water
    2½    cups vodka

Bring water and sugar to a boil. Cool and mix with all other ingredients in a tightly sealed jar. Leave for **1 month**, shaking occasionally. Strain and then pass through a paper filter into a jar and seal tightly. Store in a cool, dark place for **4 months**.

# Blackberry Brandy

This liqueur is excellent served any time of the day.

    2½    cups blackberries
    2½    cups dry brandy

Crush blackberries and put into a tightly sealed jar with brandy. Leave for **20 days**, shaking twice daily during the first week. Strain and pass through a paper filter into a glass jar and seal tightly. Store in a dark place for **7 months**.

# Blackberry Liqueur

This liqueur has a beautiful purple color with a superb bouquet.

2½   cups blackberries
1½   cups sugar
2     cups brandy

Crush and put berries and 1 cup brandy in a glass jar. Cover tightly, shake, and let steep for **1 week**. Strain through a cloth, squeezing to remove all juice. Repeat without squeezing to remove haze. Add last cup of brandy and sugar. Leave for **2 weeks**.

# Blackberries in Liqueur

Fresh ripe blackberries steeped in a lightly spiced liqueur make for a fine tasting after dinner drink.

1¼   lbs. blackberries
½"   piece cinnamon stick
6     whole cloves
1     lemon - yellow sliced peel only
1¾   cups sugar
2     cups vodka

Place berries, sugar and half the vodka in a tightly sealed jar and set in the sun until all the sugar is dissolved. Then add remaining ingredients. Close jar and put in a cool, dark place for **6 months**. Shake gently a few times during the first week.  Strain and enjoy!

**Extract Recipe:**

- 1 cup sugar
- ½ cup water
- 1 bottle Blackberry Extract
- 3 cups vodka

# How To Serve:

### Blackberry Cooler

Pour over ice in a tall glass:

- 1½ oz. blackberry liqueur
- ½ oz. lemon juice

Fill with sparkling water.

### Poopdeck

Shake with ice and strain into glass:

- ¼ oz. blackberry liqueur
- ¼ oz. port
- ½ oz. brandy

Excellent when served "on the rocks!"

Try as a dessert topping over ice cream.

# Black Currant Brandy

An aromatic fruit brandy with a hearty taste. Excellent as an apartif!

| | |
|---|---|
| ¾ | cup black currants |
| 3 | cups brandy |

Place the black currants and brandy in a glass jar, seal tightly and store in a cool, dark place for **8 months**. Strain and enjoy!

**Extract Recipe:**

| | |
|---|---|
| 2 | cups sugar |
| 1 | cup water |
| 1 | bottle Black Currant Extract |
| 2 | cups vodka |

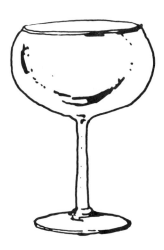

# Blueberry Liqueur

This full bodied liqueur is excellent as an after dinner drink.

| | |
|---|---|
| 4 | cups blueberries |
| 5 | whole cloves |
| ½ | tsp. whole coriander seed |
| 1 | cup sugar |
| ½ | cup water |
| 2½ | cups vodka |

Mash berries in a glass jar and add vodka, water, whole cloves and whole coriander seed. Cover and let stand for **10 days**. Strain mixture through a strainer. Add sugar and shake until dissolved. Wait 24 hours and pour through a cloth. Let stand until clear.

## How To Serve:

### Blue Moon

Pour over ice in a cocktail glass:

| | |
|---|---|
| 1 | oz. blueberry liqueur |
| 1 | oz. vodka |
| 1 | oz. orange juice |

# Cafe Sport

A mild flavoured liqueur with a hint of coffee, enhanced by a blend of vanilla.

| | |
|---|---|
| 2″ | piece vanilla bean |
| ¼ | cup instant coffee |
| 2 | cups sugar |
| 1½ | cups water |
| 2 | cups dark rum |

Cut the vanilla bean into 3 pieces. Add to the sugar and water, and boil for 15 minutes. Let cool. Dissolve the coffee in ½ cup of boiling water, mixing with the sugar mixture and rum. Seal and shake well. Let sit for **2 weeks**.

## Extract Recipe:

| | |
|---|---|
| 1½ | cups sugar |
| ¾ | cup water |
| 5 | T. Glucose Solids |
| 1 | bottle Cafe Sport Extract |
| 2½ | cups vodka |

## How To Serve:

Cafe Sport can be substituted for moka in many drinks.

# Camomile Liqueur

Made with a base of camomile flowers, this liqueur is a mild soothing digestive, especially welcome in the evening after a large dinner.

- 1½ cups camomile flowers
- 1 lemon - scraped outer peel only (no white pith)
- 1 pinch carrot seeds
- 1½ cups sugar
- 1½ cups water
- 2 cups vodka

Place camomile flowers, sliced lemon peel and vodka in an air tight jar and leave for **2 weeks**. Dissolve the sugar in boiling water, let cool, and add to contents of jar. Shake well and let stand for **2 weeks**. Filter through cheesecloth and store in a cool dark place for **2½ months**.

## How To Serve:

### Camomile Tea

To hot tea add:
- 1 oz. Camomile Liqueur

# Cantaloupe Liqueur

A different and delicious liqueur. Its inherent flavour is mildly sweet with a pleasant tang.

| | |
|---|---|
| 2 | cups ripe cantaloupe cut into ½″ pieces |
| ½ | cup sugar |
| ¼ | cup water |
| ½ | lemon - scraped outer peel only (no white pith) |
| 2 | cups vodka |

Place fruit pieces and sliced lemon peel in the vodka and steep for **1 week**. Strain and squeeze the softened fruit to extract as much juice as possible. Dissolve the sugar in boiling water and let cool. Add to vodka mixture and store in a cool, dark place for **3 weeks**.

Add sugar to the squeezed out fruit and use as a dessert topping or eat plain.

For variation, substitute cantaloupe for papaya, mango or honeydew melon.

## How To Serve:

### Tebor

Pour over ice:
| | |
|---|---|
| 1 | oz. Cantaloupe Liqueur |
| | fill with milk |

Excellent when served "on the rocks."

# Caraway Liqueur

This fragrant liqueur has characteristics similar to kummel and akvavit. It is great as a before or after dinner drink.

| | |
|---|---|
| 2 | T. caraway seeds |
| 4 | whole cloves |
| 1 | tsp. anise seeds |
| ½ | tsp. coriander seeds |
| 2½ | cups sugar |
| 1¾ | cups water |
| 2½ | cups vodka |

Put all ingredients except the sugar and water in a tightly sealed jar for **2 weeks**. Then, dissolve the sugar in boiling water, let cool and add to the contents of jar. Shake and let stand for **2 more weeks**. Then strain through a paper filter into a glass jar and seal tightly. Leave for **8 months**.

# Cherry Brandy

This brandy is light, fruity and fairly dry.

3 cups cherries
½ cup sugar
3 cups brandy

Pierce cherries with a fork, and with 2 cups brandy, put in a glass jar. Leave for **1 month**, then strain. Add remaining brandy and sugar. Stir well, to dissolve the sugar and let sit until clear.

# Cherry Liqueur, Black

The delightful taste of this liqueur matches its appealing deep red cherry colour.

2½ cups pitted black cherries
10 crushed cherry pits
10 cherry leaves
5 whole cloves
½" piece cinnamon stick
1 lemon - sliced peel only
1 cup sugar
3 cups vodka

Crush the pitted cherries and mix with all the other ingredients. Place in a tightly sealed jar and leave in the sun for **1 week**, shaking occasionally. Then store in a cool, dark place for **5 more weeks**. Strain the mixture through cheesecloth until clear, into a glass jar, tightly sealing it. Return to the cool, dark place for **6 more months**.

# Cherry Leaf Liqueur

This pale yellow liqueur is particularly delicious as an after dinner drink.

    75    black cherry leaves
    ½     lemon - sliced peel only
    ½     cup sugar
    3½    cups sweet white wine
    2     cups vodka

Put the cherry leaves, sugar, wine and lemon peel in a tightly sealed jar. Leave for **2 months**, shaking occasionally. Then add the vodka and store again for **20 days**. Strain through a paper filter into a glass jar and seal tightly. Let stand for **6 more months**.

# Cherry Liqueur

An excellent drink to end a meal.

    2     lbs. sweet cherries
    ½     lemon - sliced peel only
    3½    cups sugar
    4     cups dry white vermouth

Pull the stems off half the cherries and cut off the other stems near the fruit. Place all the ingredients in a tightly sealed jar and leave for **1 month**, shaking occasionally. Then strain through paper filter into a glass jar and seal tightly. Set in a cool, dark place for **6 months**.

**Extract Recipe:**

½   cup sugar
¼   cup water
1   bottle Cherry Brandy Extract
3½  cups brandy

# How To Serve:

**Merry Widow**

Shake with ice and serve with a cherry:

½   cherry liqueur
½   marashino

**Up Tom's**

Pour over ice:

1/3  cherry brandy
1/3  french vermouth
1/3  brandy
Garnish with an orange peel.

**Zombie**

In a tall glass with ice, add:

1   oz. dark rum
1   oz. light rum
½   oz. cherry brandy
½   oz. triple sec
½   oz. lemon juice
½   oz. simple syrup
½   oz. orange juice
Fill glass with Soda Water and 7-Up.
Float ¼ oz. over proof rum.

# Chocolate Liqueur

A pleasantly sweet liqueur excellent by itself or as a topping for dessert.

|     |                                              |
|-----|----------------------------------------------|
| 4   | tsp. pure chocolate extract (used for baking) |
| 1   | tsp. pure vanilla extract                    |
| 1   | cup sugar                                    |
| ½   | cup water                                    |
| 3   | cups vodka                                   |

Dissolve the sugar in boiling water and let cool. Then mix all the ingredients together in a tightly sealed jar. Store in a cool dark place for **2 weeks**.

# Coconut Liqueur

A dry liqueur having a rich bouquet which is touched with the sweet fragrance of the coconut. It is best served after dinner.

|     |                         |
|-----|-------------------------|
| 2   | cups fresh coconut meat |
| 4   | coriander leaves        |
| 4   | juniper berries         |
| 2½  | cups brandy             |
| 1   | cup vodka               |

Cut the coconut into small pieces and add to rest of ingredients in a glass jar. Seal tightly and leave for **3 weeks** in a cool, dark place. Gently shake from time to time. Then strain through a paper filter into a glass jar and seal tightly. Return to the cool, dark place and leave for **3 months**.

# Clear Orange Liqueur

A colorless liqueur delicately flavoured with orange.

## Extract Recipe:

| | |
|---|---|
| 1 | cup sugar |
| ½ | cup water |
| 1 | bottle Orange Triple Dry Extract |
| 3 | cups vodka |

# How To Serve:

## Bomber

Shake with ice and strain into a glass:

| | |
|---|---|
| 1 | jigger cognac |
| 1/3 | jigger clear orange liqueur |
| 1/3 | jigger anisette |
| 2/3 | jigger vodka |

## Sidecar Cocktail

Shake with ice and strain into glass:

1/3 clear orange liqueur
1/3 brandy
1/3 lemon juice

# Coffee Liqueur

Made with a base of espresso coffee, this liqueur is best served after dinner.

|       |                           |
|-------|---------------------------|
| ¾     | cup strong espresso coffee |
| ¼     | tsp. crushed vanilla bean |
| 1     | lemon - sliced peel only  |
| 1¾    | cups sugar                |
| 1¾    | cups water                |
| 3     | cups vodka                |

Slice the lemon peel into thin strips. Put the peel, coffee and vanilla in a tightly sealed jar for **1 week**. Dissolve the sugar in boiling water and let cool. Add the syrup and vodka to contents of jar. Let sit for another week, shaking occasionally. Then strain the mixture into a glass jar and seal tightly. Store in a cool, dark place for **1 month**.

## How To Serve:

### Double Coffee

To hot coffee add:

|   |                        |
|---|------------------------|
| 1 | oz. Coffee Liqueur     |
|   | cream if desired       |

Excellent when served with cream on the rocks.

# Creme De Cacao Liqueur

A mild, rich, sweet liqueur which has a full-bodied chocolate flavour.

## Extract Recipe:

| | |
|---|---|
| 2 | cups sugar |
| 1 | cup water |
| 6 | T. Glucose Solids |
| 1 | bottle Cocoa Extract |
| 2 | cups vodka |

## How To Serve:

### Alexander

Shake with ice and strain into glass:

| | |
|---|---|
| 1 | oz. creme de cacao |
| 1 | oz. gin |
| 1 | oz. sweet cream |

### Aunt Jemima

Float:

| | |
|---|---|
| 1/3 | creme de cacao |
| 1/3 | brandy |
| 1/3 | benedictine |

### Cafe Cocktail

To hot coffee add:

| | |
|---|---|
| ½ | oz. creme de cacao |
| ½ | oz. cognac |
| 1 | tsp. sugar |

# Creme De Menthe Liqueur

This liqueur has an appealing mint flavour. Even though it is commonly green, it can also be found in a variety of other colours.

1½    cups crushed fresh mint leaves
1     cup sugar
½     cup water
4     T. Glucose Solids
3     cups vodka

Put leaves in a large jar and cover with vodka. Steep for **48 hours** and strain. Boil sugar, water and Glucose Solids until dissolved. When cool, add to mint liqueur and leave until clear.

## Extract Recipe:

2     cups sugar
1     cup water
1     bottle Green Mint Extract
2     cups vodka

# How To Serve:

## American Beauty
Shake with ice and strain into a glass:
¼     oz. creme de menthe
½     oz. brandy
½     oz. dry vermouth
¼     oz. grenadine
½     oz. orange juice

## Grasshopper

Shake with ice and strain into glass:

$\frac{3}{4}$ oz. creme de menthe
$\frac{3}{4}$ oz. creme de cacao
$\frac{3}{4}$ oz. sweet cream

## Shrimps'

Shake with ice and strain into a glass:

1 part creme de menthe
2 parts brandy

## White Lady

Shake with ice and strain into glass:

2/3 cointreau
1/6 creme de menthe
1/6 brandy

# Cream Marsala

A creamy rich liqueur that can be served as is, but is particularly delicious when served as a topping over desserts.

| | |
|---|---|
| 5 | egg yolks |
| 1 | cup milk |
| 1½ | cups sugar |
| ½" | piece vanilla bean |
| 1 | cup marsala wine |
| 1 | cup vodka |

Combine the egg yolks and sugar in the top of a glass double boiler or enamel pan. Slowly add the milk, half the marsala and the vanilla, blending with a whisk to avoid lumps. Bring the mixture to a boil and simmer for 5 minutes. Continue to stir. Remove from the heat, cool to lukewarm — still stirring — and add the remaining ingredients. Take out the vanilla bean, and pour into a tightly sealed jar. Shake well and store in a cool, dark place for **2 months**. If the jar is left tightly closed in a cool, dark place, the liqueur will keep indefinitely, as the alcohol acts as a preservative.

# Curacao

This liqueur is similar to cointreau, but is red in colour.

>     4    oranges
>     1    cup liquid honey
>     3    cups bourbon

Remove the outer peel from the oranges without any of the white pith. Steep the peel in the bourbon for **1 month**, strain and add honey. Let stand until clear.

### Extract Recipe:

>     1    cup sugar
>     ½    cup water
>     1    bottle Orange Red Curacao Extract
>     3    cups vodka

## How To Serve:

### Curacao Tea

Add to hot tea:

>     1    oz. curacao
>     1    tsp. lemon juice
>          lemon slice

# Drambuie

A golden liqueur blended with different herbs and honey. A favourite among many.

## Extract Recipe:

½     cup sugar
¼     cup water
1     bottle Lorbuis Extract
3½    cups scotch

## How To Serve:

### Rusty Nail

Pour over ice in a glass:

½     oz. drambuie
1     oz. scotch whiskey

### Sun Rise

Fill a glass with ice and add:

2     oz. drambuie
1     oz. dry vermouth
3     oz. orange juice
      juice of half a lemon

For a tastier coffee, add 1 oz. drambuie.

# Egg Liqueur

## like Advockaat

A thick, sweet egg and brandy liqueur. Delicious by itself or added to eggnog.

| | |
|---|---|
| 8 | egg yolks |
| ¼ | tsp. vanilla extract |
| 2 | cups sweetened condensed milk |
| 1 | cup sugar |
| 2½ | cups brandy |

Beat egg yolks, vanilla extract and sugar until a pale yellow color. While beating, slowly add condensed milk. Add brandy and stir thoroughly. Put in a tightly sealed bottle and store in a cool, dark place for **one year**. After opening, the shelf life is about 5 months, if kept in a cool dark place.

# Eggnog Liqueur

A sweet dessert liqueur which is rich and nutritious.

| | |
|---|---|
| 2 | cups milk |
| 2 | cups sugar |
| 5 | egg yolks |
| ½″ | piece vanilla bean |
| 1½ | cups dry marsala wine |
| 1 | cup vodka |

Bring the milk to a boil with vanilla bean, remove from heat and stir in half the sugar until dissolved. Cool. Blend the egg yolks into the rest of sugar, and little by little, add the marsala and vodka, beating well with a whisk. Remove the vanilla bean from the milk and slowly add the milk to the other mixture, beating all the while with a whisk. Continue beating for a few minutes longer after all the ingredients have been combined. Then strain the liqueur into a jar, seal tightly and store in a cool, dark place for **2 months**. If the bottle is left tightly closed in a cool, dark place the liqueur will keep indefinitely, since the alcohol acts as a preservative.

# Four Fruits Liqueur

This is not only exquisite and delightful as a liqueur, but is also refreshing when served "on the rocks."

| | |
|---|---|
| 2 | cups strawberries |
| 2 | cups raspberries |
| 2 | cups gooseberries |
| 2 | cups huckleberries, elderberries, or bilberries |
| 1½ | cups sugar |
| 3 | cups vodka |

Crush the fruit in a bowl, mix well with the sugar and place in the refrigerator for **5 hours**. Transfer the pulp and juices into a jar and add the vodka. Seal tightly and store for **3 weeks**. Then strain through cheesecloth until clear, into a glass jar. Seal tightly and store in a cool, dark place for 6 months.

# Galliano

This bright yellow, herbal liqueur adds a distinctive taste to many drinks.

## Extract Recipe:

|   |   |
|---|---|
| 1 | cup sugar |
| ½ | cup water |
| 5 | T. Glucose Solids |
| 1 | bottle Yellow Genepy Extract |
| 3 | cups vodka |

# How To Serve:

## Golden Cadallac

Shake with ice and strain:

|   |   |
|---|---|
| 1 | oz. galliano |
| ½ | oz. white cacao |
| 1 | oz. cream |

## Harvey Wallbanger

Fill glass with ice and add:

|   |   |
|---|---|
| 1 | oz. vodka |

Fill glass with orange juice. Float ½ oz. galliano. Garnish with a cherry and orange slice.

# Gooseberry Liqueur

This liqueur has a rich, appetizing red purple colour and a lovely, full fruit flavour.

3 cups ripe gooseberries
1 cup sugar
2½ cups vodka

Crush the gooseberries and put them into a tightly sealed jar with sugar and vodka. Let sit in a warm place until the sugar dissolves, shaking occasionally. When the sugar has dissolved, filter the mixture through cheese-cloth and a paper filter. Store in a cool, dark place in a tightly sealed jar for **4 months**.

# Grapefruit Liqueur

A sweet, unusual liqueur, welcome anytime of the day.

2 grapefruits - scraped outer peel only (no white pith)
½ cup sugar
¼ cup water
3 cups brandy

Cut peel into pieces and steep in brandy for **10 days**. Dissolve the sugar in boiling water and let cool. Add to brandy mixture and store in a cool dark place for **1 week**. Strain and enjoy!

For variation add scraped, sliced orange peel as well.

# Green Grape Liqueur

The fine grape taste of this fruit liqueur makes it a welcome drink any time of the day.

3½ cups green grapes
½ cup sugar
4 whole cloves
1 T. coriander seeds
½" piece cinnamon stick
1 cup vodka
2 cups brandy

Put the vodka, brandy, cloves, cinnamon and coriander in a tightly sealed jar for **2 weeks.** Then, stirring constantly, heat the grapes over very low heat until the skins pop open. Pour them into a colander lined with cheesecloth and press out 2 cups of the juice. Dissolve the sugar in the warm juice, cool and add to the contents of the jar. Mix well but carefully and let the jar stand for **1 month.** Then strain through a colander and paper filter into a glass jar. Seal tightly and store in a cool, dark place for **7 months.**

# Green Grape Vermouth

This sweet liqueur is excellent as an apertif.

| | |
|---|---|
| 2 | cups green grape liqueur from preceding recipe |
| 3 | lemon verbena leaves |
| 1½ | cups sugar |
| 1 | cup vodka |
| 2 | cups dry white vermouth |

Stir the sugar into the grape liqueur, bring to a boil, and simmer over low heat for 4 minutes. Cool and pour into a tightly sealed jar along with the vermouth, vodka and lemon verbena. Mix well and leave for **4 months**, shaking occasionally. Then, strain through cheesecloth into a glass jar and seal well. The liqueur may be served immediately, but the bouquet is improved if it sits a few months longer.

# Green Tomato Liqueur

A classic and unusual liqueur. The reaction of those who try it, is one of surprise and delight.

| | |
|---|---|
| 1 | lb. green tomatoes |
| 4 | tomato leaves |
| 6 | lemon verbena leaves |
| 6 | sage leaves |
| 3″ | sprig of rosemary |
| 3 | cups sugar |
| ¾ | cup water |
| 1 | cup brandy |
| 2 | cups vodka |

Crush tomatoes in a bowl with 2 cups sugar. Put into a tightly sealed jar and add all other ingredients except vodka, water and rest of sugar. Store in a dark place for **4 days**, shaking occasionally. Dissolve the remaining sugar in boiling water and cool. Add this syrup and the vodka to the jar, shake well, and set in a cool, dark place for **10 days**. Then strain through a colander and paper filter into a glass jar. Seal tightly and set in a dark place for **3 months**.

## Huckleberry, Elderberry or Bilberry Liqueur

This sweet fruit liqueur is delicious after a large dinner. An excellent complement to many desserts.

5    cups huckleberries, elderberries or bilberries
2    cups sugar
¼    lemon, sliced peel only
2    cups vodka

Put all ingredients in a tightly sealed jar and set in the sun for **1 month.** Then transfer to a cool, dark place for **4 months.** Strain before serving.

## Huckleberries, Elderberries or Bilberries in Liqueur

An inviting rose coloured liqueur especially appropriate after a fine dinner.

4    cups huckleberries, elderberries or bilberries
3    whole cloves
¼    tsp. tarragon
½    lemon, yellow sliced peel only
1    cup sweet white wine
2    cups vodka

Combine all the ingredients in a tightly sealed jar and leave for **4 months.**

# Irish Cream

This rich, creamy liqueur is an old time favorite. Excellent to sit back and relax with.

3      eggs
½      cup sweetened condensed milk
3      T. chocolate syrup
1      pinch instant coffee
1      cup table cream
1      cup Irish Whiskey or Scotch

One of the easiest liqueurs to make. Simply put all the ingredients in a blender and whip thoroughly. Pour into a glass bottle and keep in the refrigerator. I suggest you drink this liqueur before the date shown on the fresh ingredients.

## How To Serve:

### B-52

Float in a liqueur glass:

1/3   moka
1/3   Irish cream
1/3   orange brandy

For a smooth coffee, add 1 oz. Irish cream.

Tastes great when served "on the rocks".

# Juniper Liqueur

This liqueur has a taste which is reminiscent of gin, although it is a bit sweeter.

| | |
|---|---|
| 3 | cups juniper berries |
| 1½ | cups sugar |
| 1½ | cups water |
| 2 | cups vodka |

Put the juniper berries and vodka in a tightly sealed jar. Let sit for **1 month**. Dissolve the sugar in boiling water and cool. Strain the berry mixture through a paper filter and add the sugar syrup. Mix well and store in a glass jar, tightly sealed. Let stand in a cool, dark place for **7 months**.

## Extra!

When a recipe uses a vanilla bean, do not throw it away! Just let it dry, and it can be used over and over again.

# Kirsh

This liqueur is strong, not very sweet, and clear in colour. One of the oldest liqueurs.

4½   cups unpitted sour cherries
1     cup sugar
4     cups vodka

Cut up the cherries and remove the pits. Wrap the pits in a cloth and smash with a hammer. Put the cherries, pits, and vodka in a tightly sealed jar. Let steep for **4 weeks**, and then strain. Add the sugar and shake until it is dissolved. Let stand for **1 week**.

### Extract Recipe:

1     bottle Kirsh Extract
4     cups vodka

## How To Serve:

### Black Jack

Frappe with fine ice:

1     pony kirsh
1     dash brandy
1     pony coffee

### Kirsh and Cassis

1     part Cassis
½     part Kirsh
Top with soda water

# Kummel

A strong, caraway seed flavour distinguishes this clear, dry liqueur.

| | |
|---|---|
| 2 | T. caraway seeds |
| 3 | tsp. fennel seeds |
| 1½ | tsp. cumin |
| 1 | cup simple syrup |
| 1 | fifth vodka |

Crush the caraway and fennel seeds. Add to the cumin and vodka. Steep for **1½ weeks,** then strain out the seeds. Add the sugar syrup and enjoy!

## Extract Recipe:

| | |
|---|---|
| 1 | cup sugar |
| ½ | cup water |
| 1 | bottle Kummel Extract |
| 3 | cups vodka |

# How To Serve:

## Skipper Rick

| | |
|---|---|
| 1 | pint Jamaica Rum |
| ½ | pint Cognac |
| 2 | oz. Kummel |
| 2 | oz. Benedictine |
| | Rind of lemon and orange |
| 3 | pints piping hot water |
| | sweeten to taste |

# Lemon and Orange Liqueur

A fairly dry liqueur with a pleasant citrus bouquet.

|       |                                  |
|-------|----------------------------------|
| 4     | oranges, orange part of peel only |
| 4     | lemons, yellow part of peel only  |
| ¾     | cup sugar                        |
| 4     | cups brandy                      |
| 1     | cup sweet sparkling wine         |
| 1     | cup vodka                        |

Slice the lemon and orange peel and add to all other ingredients in a glass jar. Let sit for **3 months**. Then strain through a paper filter into a glass jar and seal tightly. Store in a cool, dark place for **6 months**.

# Milk and Cherry Liqueur

This creamy smooth liqueur is nutritious as well as very tasty.

| | |
|---|---|
| 1½ | cups pitted sweet cherries |
| 2½ | cups sugar |
| 1 | whole lemon |
| ¼ | tsp. crushed vanilla bean |
| 2½ | cups milk |
| 2½ | cups vodka |

Cut half of the lemon into thin slices and use just the peel of the other half (only the yellow), cut into thin strips. Put these, along with all the other ingredients, into a tightly sealed jar and leave for **3 weeks**. Shake the jar twice daily during this period. Then strain through a colander and cloth into a glass jar and seal tightly. Store in a cool, dark place for **6 months**. If the bottle is left tightly closed in a cool, dark, place, the liqueur will keep indefinitely, since the alcohol acts as a preservative.

# Moka

A coffee liqueur with a very pleasing taste. A favourite dessert style drink.

½   cup instant coffee
4   cups sugar
3½  cups water
1   vanilla bean
1   26 oz. bottle of tequilla or brandy

Boil the coffee, sugar and water together for 8 minutes. Cool completely. Add the vodka and vanilla bean and pour into a large glass container. Store in a cool, dark place for **2 weeks** before serving.

**Extract Recipe:**

1½  cups brown sugar
¾   cups water
5   T. Glucose Solids
1   bottle Moka Extract
2½  cups vodka

## How To Serve:

**Accident**

Pour over ice:

½   oz. moka
1   oz. southern comfort

## Black Russian

Pour over ice:

    ¾   oz. moka
    1½  oz. vodka

## Dirty Mother

Pour over ice:

    ¾   oz. moka
    1   oz. tequilla
    Fill glass with cream.

## Grumps Best

Pour over ice:

    1   oz. moka
    ½   oz. cointreau
    Fill glass with cream.

## Rootbeer

Pour over ice into a tall glass:

    1   oz. moka
    1   oz. galliano
    Fill glass with 7-Up and Soda Water.
    Float ½ oz. moka.

# Mountain Ash Liqueur

An unusual liqueur made from the edible fruit of the Mountain Ash. It has a delicious taste and an appealing aroma.

3 cups mountain ash fruit
3 whole cloves
½ inch piece cinnamon stick

1 lemon, yellow sliced peel only
1 cup sugar
2 cups vodka

Place all the ingredients in a tightly sealed jar and leave for **6 months**. Expose the jar to the sun for the first week, shaking frequently. Then set aside in a cool, dark place for the remaining time. Then strain through a cloth into a glass jar, seal well and store in a cool, dark place for **4 more months**.

# Orange Brandy

A brandy based liqueur flavoured with orange and herbs. An excellent after dinner drink, but is also ideal for flavouring certain desserts.

**Extract Recipe:**

| | |
|---|---|
| 1 | cup sugar |
| ½ | cup water |
| 5 | T. Glucose Solids |
| 1 | bottle Orange Brandy Extract |
| 3 | cups brandy |

## How To Serve:

**Monti Cristo — Excellent!**

To hot coffee add:

| | |
|---|---|
| 1 | oz. orange brandy |
| ¾ | oz. moka |

Top with whipped cream and a cherry.

**French Coffee**

To hot coffee add:

| | |
|---|---|
| 1 | oz. brandy |
| ¾ | oz. orange brandy |

Top with whipped cream.

# Oranges in Liqueur

Sweet mature oranges, steeped in liqueur to create a taste reminiscent of cointreau.

| | |
|---|---|
| 5 | medium naval oranges |
| 3 | whole cloves |
| ½ | inch piece cinnamon stick |
| 2 | cups sugar |
| 3 | cups vodka |

Stab the oranges with a fork in a number of places and place them in a large tightly sealed glass jar. Add remaining ingredients. Seal well, and let steep for **6 months**, shaking once a week. At the end of this time, remove the oranges and strain the liqueur through a cloth. Wash the glass jar thoroughly and return the oranges and liqueur to it. Close and let stand for **2 more weeks** before serving.

The oranges may be served separately to make a delightful dessert.

# Orange Liqueur, Dry

A refreshing, full orange flavour.

    2     cups fresh orange juice
    1     orange, sliced orange peel only
    2     lemons, sliced yellow peel only
    4     whole cloves
    ½     inch piece cinnamon stick
    1     tangerine, quartered
    ½     cup sugar
    2     cups vodka

Combine all the ingredients in a tightly sealed jar. Store in a cool, dark place for **6 months**, shaking occasionally. Strain through a colander and then a cloth into a glass jar. Seal tightly and store in a cool, dark place for **5 months**.

# Orange Liqueur, Sweet

A sweet citrus liqueur made of fresh squeezed orange juice. A perfect dessert liqueur.

    2½    cups fresh orange juice
    ½     cup lemon juice
    3     lemons, sliced peel only
    ¼     tsp. caraway seeds
    2     cups sugar
    1½    cups vodka

Strain the orange juice into a tightly sealed jar, along with the remaining ingredients. Let sit for **5 months**, shaking occasionally. Then strain through cheesecloth into a glass jar. Seal tightly and set aside in a cool, dark place for **5 months**.

# Orange and Lemon Liqueur

This liqueur has a rich golden colour and can be served at almost any time of the day.

| | |
|---|---|
| 4 | oranges, sliced orange peel only |
| 2 | lemons, sliced yellow peel only |
| ½ | lime, sliced green peel only |
| 1½ | cups sugar |
| 1½ | cups water |
| 2 | cups vodka |

Dissolve the sugar in boiling water. Cool this syrup and place in a tightly closed jar, along with all the other ingredients. Let sit for **10 days** shaking occasionally. Then strain through cheesecloth into a glass jar and seal tightly. Leave for **5 months** in a cool, dark place.

# Orange and Pear Liqueur

A sweet, mellow liqueur which is also delicious as a dessert sauce.

| | |
|---|---|
| 2 | oranges, peeled |
| 2 | pears, peeled and cored |
| 1¼ | cups sugar |
| 2 | cups vodka |

Cut the pears into slices and place them in a tightly sealed jar with the sugar. Expose to the sun for **1 week**, shaking occasionally. Then cut the oranges into wedges and add to the jar along with the vodka. Mix and let stand for **4 weeks**, shaking occasionally. At the end of this time, strain the mixture through a cloth into a glass jar and seal. Store in a cool, dark place for **7 months**.

# Peach Liqueur

Two fantastic recipes!

This is a very light, delicately flavoured liqueur.

| | |
|---|---|
| 9 | small peaches |
| 1½ | cups sugar |
| ½ | cup honey |
| 3 | cups vodka |

Peel and cut the peaches into small sections. Put in a glass jar with the vodka and leave for **1 week**, shaking frequently. Strain and add sugar and honey. Stir well and leave for **1 week**.


This fascinating and classic liqueur is made from the leaves of the peach tree.

| | |
|---|---|
| 70 | peach leaves |
| ½ | lemon, sliced yellow peel |
| ½ | cup sugar |
| 3 | cups sparkling white wine, semi-sweet |
| 1½ | cups vodka |

Put all ingredients in a tightly sealed jar. Leave for **6 weeks**, shaking occasionally. Then strain, and store in a tightly sealed jar for **9 months**.

# Pear Liqueur

A mild, sweet liqueur that can be served any time of the day.

|     |                                |
|-----|--------------------------------|
| 3   | pears                          |
| 2   | cups sugar                     |
| ½   | cup water                      |
| 1   | orange, sliced yellow peel only |
| 3   | whole cloves                   |
| ½   | tsp. whole coriander           |
| ½   | tsp. ground cinnamon           |
| 1   | whole peppercorn               |
| 2   | cups vodka                     |

Remove seeds and dice the pears. Put in a glass jar along with the spices, vodka and orange peel. Cover and leave for **2 weeks**. Dissolve the sugar in the water and add to the strained mixture. Leave for **2 weeks**.

## Extract Recipe:

|     |                    |
|-----|--------------------|
| 2   | cups sugar         |
| 1   | cup water          |
| 1   | bottle Pear Extract |
| 2   | cups vodka         |

# Peppermint Liqueur

So refreshing when served in a small glass or when poured over ice cream.

| | |
|---|---|
| 13 | T. fresh, well crumpled peppermint or |
| 6 | T. dried peppermint leaves |
| 1 | cup sugar |
| ½ | cup water |
| 1 | tsp. glycerine (optional, but nice for sipping) |
| 3 | cups vodka |

With fresh or dried leaves: steep the leaves in vodka for **10 days**, shaking the bottle occasionally. Strain and filter, pressing all the juices from the leaves. Leave for **2 weeks**. Dissolve the sugar in boiling water and let cool. Combine sugar syrup with remaining ingredients. Shake well. Let mature for **2 weeks** in a cool, dark place.

If globules of oil form on the surface of the liqueur, remove by dabbing them gently with a paper towel.

For a variation, substitute mint or spearmint for peppermint.

# Pineapple Liqueur

This sweet liqueur's pleasant fruit bouquet gives only a hint of its rich fruit base.

    3    cups fresh pineapple meat
    1    cup sugar
    ½    inch piece vanilla bean
    1½   cups vodka

Peel the pineapple and chop the flesh into small cubes. Place in a tightly sealed jar along with rest of the ingredients. Leave for **1 week**, shaking twice daily to help mix ingredients. Then strain through a colander and cloth into a glass jar. Seal tightly and let sit for **6 months.**

# Pineapple Rum

A dry and appealingly robust liqueur.

    2    cups fresh pineapple meat
    3½   cups rum (pref. light)

Peel pineapple and chop into small pieces. Mix with rum and store in a tightly sealed jar for **3 weeks.** Strain through a colander and cloth into a jar and seal well. Store in a cool, dark place for **2 months**.

# Plum Liqueur

A pleasant, delicate, pale yellow fruit liqueur with a flowery aroma.

2    lbs. yellow plums
¼    tsp. crushed vanilla bean
½    lemon, yellow sliced peel only
2    cups sugar
3    cups rum

Halve and pit the plums. Put in a glass jar with remaining ingredients, sealing tightly. Let stand for **4 months**, shaking occasionally to dissolve sugar. Strain and enjoy!

The plums chilled, make a delicious dessert.

# Plums In Liqueur

Sweet prune plums steeped in liqueur make an excellent digestive.

1    lb. whole, sweet prune plums
4    whole cloves
½″    piece cinnamon stick
1    pinch caraway seeds
1    cup sugar
2    cups vodka

Place all ingredients in an airtight glass jar and leave for **6 months**. Shake occasionally during first **3 months**. Strain off spices and plums before serving liqueur. Plums may be sugared and served separately for dessert.

**Extract Recipe:**

1    cup sugar
½    cup water
1    bottle Yellow Plum Extract
3    cups vodka

## Pomegranate Liqueur

A delightfully aromatic liqueur. It has an appealing deep red colour and a superb, rich fruit taste.

2    cups pomegranate juice
     (about 6 pomegranates)
1    tsp. caraway seeds
1    T. hibiscus petals
¾    cup sugar
2½   cups vodka

Squeeze the pomegranates, straining the juice. Pour the juice along with remaining ingredients into a tightly sealed jar. Store for **1 month**, shaking occasionally to help mix the ingredients. Then strain through cheesecloth into a glass jar and seal tightly. Set aside in a cool, dark place for **5 months**.

# Raspberry Liqueur

This favourite liqueur has an inviting rose colour, a full fruit taste, and is delightful at almost any time.

    3    cups raspberries
    15   cherry leaves
    2½   cups sugar
    ½    lemon, sliced yellow peel only
    2½   cups vodka

Put all of the ingredients in a tightly sealed jar and put in the sun for **1 month**, shaking occasionally. Then place in a cool, dark place for **5 more months**. Strain through a colander and cloth into a glass jar and seal well. Return to the cool, dark place for **1 more month**.

# Raspberries in Liqueur

Sweet ripe raspberries steeped in a lightly spiced liqueur create a delicious after dinner drink, with a lovely pale rose colour.

    3    cups red raspberries
    15   cherry leaves
    ½    inch piece cinnamon stick
    2    whole cloves
    ¼    lemon, sliced yellow peel only
    ½    cup sugar
    2    cups vodka

Place all the ingredients in a tightly sealed jar and leave for **5 months**. After this period, the liqueur can be strained off and bottled to be served by itself. Sprinkled with a little sugar, the raspberries may be served for dessert.

**Extract Recipe:**

      1½   cups sugar
      ¾   cup water
      1   bottle Raspberry Extract
      2½   cups vodka

# How To Serve:

### Spritzer Pitcher

Mix the juice and raspberry liqueur with ice. A very refreshing drink.

      1   can frozen lemon juice
      4   cans water
      12   oz. raspberry liqueur

Serve "on the rocks" for a refreshing drink.

# Rhubarb Liqueur

This unusual liqueur with its slightly tart after taste, is surprising and pleasant. It is best served as an aperitif.

    1     cup ground rhubarb stalk
    ½    orange, sliced peel only
    6     artichoke leaves
    1     cup sugar
    1     cup vodka
    4½  cups semi dry white wine

Put the rhubarb, orange peel and artichoke leaves with the vodka in a tightly sealed jar for **5 days**. Then dissolve the sugar in the wine and add to the contents of the jar. Mix well and let stand for another **5 days**. Strain through a colander and cloth into a glass jar and seal tightly. Set aside in a cool, dark place to mature quietly for **2 more months**.

# Rose Liqueur

This liqueur has a base of rose petals, and a bouquet and taste that are soft and flowery.

40 rose petals
1¼ cups water
1½ cups sugar
2 cups vodka

Mix the rose petals well with ½ cup of the sugar, beating for a few minutes and adding a little of the vodka. Pour the rose petal mixture into a tightly sealed jar with the rest of the vodka. Close and let stand for **10 days**, shaking a few time to help mix the ingredients. Then dissolve the rest of the sugar in boiling water. Cool completely and add to the contents of the jar. Close again, shake well, and let stand for **1 week**. At the end of this time, strain through a colander and cheesecloth into a glass jar. Seal tightly and store in a cool, dark place for **3 months.**

# Strawberry Liqueur

A sweet fruit liqueur best served after dinner or with dessert.

3 cups strawberries
¼ tsp. crushed vanilla bean
1¾ cups sugar
½ cup water
2 cups vodka

Wash and dry the strawberries quickly so they do not become saturated with water. Put all the ingredients in a tightly sealed jar for **1 month**, turning very delicately once a day. At the end of this time, strain through a colander and cheesecloth into a glass jar. Seal tightly and store in a cool, dark place for **6 months**.

The strawberries may be served as a dessert topping over ice cream or cake.

**Extra!**

# Summer Fruits Year Round

For a delicious combination of fruits, fill a big glass jar with pears (cored and chopped), oranges (peeled and cut), strawberries, cherries, or any others. Do not use blackberries or apples. For every 3 cups of fruit, add 1 cup of sugar. Cover with rum or brandy, and leave for **3 weeks.** Each time you remove some fruit, replace with an equal amount. Great over ice cream or cake!

# Tangerine Brandy Liqueur

This dry liqueur is especially welcome after a fine dinner.

    4    medium tangerines, sliced
    3½   cups brandy

Steep the tangerines and brandy in a tightly sealed jar for **1 month**. Then strain through a colander and cloth into a glass jar, sealing tightly. Store in a cool, dark place for **7 months**.

# Tangerine Liqueur, Dry

These tangerines, lightly spiced with cinnamon and cloves, have a superb aroma and a robust taste.

    3    medium tangerines, sliced
    1¼   cups water
    ½    cup sugar
    4    whole cloves
    ¼    tsp. crushed cinnamon
    1½   cups vodka

Place all ingredients in a tightly sealed jar for **4 months**, shaking occasionally. Then strain through a colander and cloth into a glass jar. Seal well and store in a cool, dark place for **5 months**. The residue in the colander may be used to make Tangerine Vermouth.

# Tangerine Liqueur, Sweet

A distinctive, pleasant bouquet and a smooth, mellow taste makes this liqueur suitable to be served at any time of the day.

> 4  medium tangerines, sliced
> 1  lemon, sliced yellow peel only
> 2  whole cloves
> 1½  cups sugar
> 2  cups vodka
> 1½  cups dry white vermouth

Put all ingredients in a tightly sealed jar for **5 months**, shaking occasionally. Then strain through cheesecloth into a glass jar. Seal tightly and store in a cool, dark place for **5 months**. The residue may be used to make Tangerine Vermouth.

# Tangerine Vermouth

The appealing sharp taste of this liqueur makes it particularly welcome as an aperitif.

> Strained residue from the preparation of Dry or Sweet Tangerine Liqueur
> 4  cups dry white vermouth

Put the residue and vermouth in a tightly sealed jar for **5 months**. Then strain through a cheesecloth into a glass jar. Seal well and store in a cool, dark place for **3 months**.

# Vanilla Liqueur

A rich, but subtle liqueur which is clear and sweet. Excellent when it is served as a topping over ice cream!

| | |
|---|---|
| 3 | vanilla beans |
| 1 | cup sugar |
| ½ | cup water |
| 3 | cups vodka |

Steep the beans in the vodka for **3 weeks** and then remove them. Then strain this mixture through a cloth. Dissolve the sugar in boiling water and cool. Add this to the vodka mixture and let sit for **1 week**.

**Extract Recipe:**

| | |
|---|---|
| 2 | cups sugar |
| 1 | cup water |
| 1 | bottle Vanilla Extract |
| 2 | cups vodka |

# Extra!

## Yukka Fluk

An excellent, nutritious summer drink. Cut the top of a watermelon off. Scrape the meat out and put into a bowl. Mix in sliced oranges, grapefruit, bananas and grapes. Add 2 cups 7-Up, and 2½ cups vodka. Pour the mixture into the hollowed out melon and put the top on. Let sit in the refrigerator for **one day**. Serve over ice and enjoy! Any other desired fruits can be used.

# Notes:

# Notes:

# Notes:

# Notes: